*The*William Morris

COLOURING BOOK

WILLIAM
MORRIS
GALLERY

HUTCHINSON

Contents

Introduction

William Morris was born in Walthamstow on the edge of Epping Forest in 1834. His love of nature developed in these early years and he spent many hours exploring the Essex countryside on his pony. One of his childhood homes, now the William Morris Gallery, has a medieval moated island in the grounds which made a great impression on him. Morris later recalled that the island was 'a sort of fairy land' for him and his brothers and sisters.

Destined for a career in the Church, his ambitions changed after he met his friend and lifelong collaborator Edward Burne-Jones at Oxford University. They became fascinated by medieval art and architecture. They were also inspired by the influential Victorian art critic John Ruskin, who celebrated the skill and hand craftsmanship of medieval artists in contrast to the dull, mass-produced wares of Victorian Britain. Ruskin was also one of the earliest champions of the Pre-Raphaelite painters, including Dante Gabriel Rossetti, who soon befriended the two young artists and encouraged their early artistic endeavours.

Morris married the Pre-Raphaelite muse Jane Burden in 1859 after she posed as an artist's model for him. Their first home together was Red House in Bexleyheath. It was designed by Morris's friend Philip Webb and now belongs to the National Trust. The design was inspired by medieval and vernacular architecture, with red bricks, turrets and hand-painted murals and furniture. The interiors at Red House were decorated by Morris and his friends, and this collaborative way of working remained important to Morris throughout his life.

The experience of building and decorating Red House inspired Morris and friends to set up the interior design business, Morris, Marshall, Faulkner & Co. 'The Firm', as it was affectionately known, claimed to offer an alternative to the shoddy, mass-produced wares of industrial Britain. Later Morris took sole ownership of The Firm, which then became Morris & Co.

Within this book you will discover many of the plants, flowers and wildlife that inspired Morris. He took his motifs from the natural world but abstracted them into complex repeat patterns. In his essay *Some Hints on Pattern Designing* he criticises designers who tried to copy nature literally, describing such patterns as 'sham-real boughs and flowers, casting sham-real shadows on your walls with little hint of anything beyond Covent Garden in them'. He wanted to evoke, rather than imitate, the natural world in his designs.

Morris also extolled the virtues of natural plant and vegetable dyes, as opposed to the synthetic dyes which had recently become more widely available. He felt they gave much richer, deeper tones. In collaboration with the master silk dyer Thomas Wardle, he revived the disappearing art of using natural dyes, particularly indigo blue and madder red.

Morris looked to historic textiles from around the world for inspiration. He became deeply knowledgeable about Indian cottons, Italian velvets, Flemish tapestries, and silks and carpets from the Middle East. Within this book, you can see some of these influences at work. *Snakeshead* (1876), for example, clearly references the Indian textiles that Morris held in high esteem. He also took inspiration from things he observed much closer to home, such as a thrush stealing strawberries from the garden of Kelmscott Manor, his idyllic country retreat in Oxfordshire. This little bird is instantly recognisable in the *Strawberry Thief* (1883), one of his most iconic and influential patterns.

Morris was an astute businessman and his textiles and wallpapers reached an international clientele. Today his designs are in houses and museum collections across Europe, America, Canada and New Zealand; there are even Morris & Co. stained glass windows in St Paul's Cathedral in Kolkata, India.

Morris's achievements as a designer are numerous and well known, but during his lifetime he was also highly regarded as a poet and writer, producing influential works such as the utopian novel *News From Nowhere* (1890). He was a political activist and one of the key figures in the early Socialist movement in Britain, campaigning for greater equality and everybody's right to live creative, fulfilling lives. For art to thrive, he believed society must change, and his political struggles were intimately connected to his experiences as a designer and craftsman. He also campaigned passionately for the preservation of historic buildings and for the protection of his boyhood haunt, Epping Forest.

Towards the end of his life in the 1890s, Morris set up his own printing press, called the Kelmscott Press, so that he could produce beautiful books. His last great work was a stunning edition of *The Complete Works of Geoffrey Chaucer* (1896), illustrated by Edward Burne-Jones, an original edition of which can be seen on display at the William Morris Gallery.

I really hope you enjoy this book and that it inspires your own creativity.

Mhairi Muncaster
Development Manager
William Morris Gallery

Have
your house
not know to
or believe to

nothing in that you do be useful, be beautiful.

Acanthus

Designed by William Morris in 1875.

Acanthus was designed as a wallpaper; thirty blocks were needed to print the pattern.

Cray

Designed by William Morris in 1884.

Cray was originally designed as a woven cloth and was based on a 17th century fabric.

Arbutus

Designed by Kathleen Kersey in 1913.

The arbutus shrub flowers in the autumn and produces large strawberry-like fruits.

Daisy

Designed by William Morris in 1864.

Daisy is more formal in style than Morris's later work. The original colourway was in shades of white, cream, green and pink.

Indian

Attributed to George Gilbert Scott, 1868.

This design takes inspiration from indienne textiles which were popular in Europe between the 17th and 19th centuries and based on traditional East Indian designs.

Thistle

Designed by John Henry Dearle circa 1890.

Sleeping Beauty

Designed by Walter Crane in 1875.

Morris & Co. took inspiration from fairy tales; the Sleeping Beauty story was also used on decorative tiles.

Horn Poppy

Designed by May Morris circa 1885.

Bird and Anemone

Designed by William Morris in 1881.

Blackthorn

Designed by John Henry Dearle in 1892.

Dearle designed many of the very popular patterns. He spent his career working for Morris & Co., starting as a Showroom Assistant and working his way up to become Art Director after Morris's death.

Compton

Designed by John Henry Dearle in 1896.

This design features poppies, tulips, speedwell, pimpernel and honeysuckle.

Willow Bough

Designed by William Morris in 1887.

Bourne

Designed by John Henry Dearle circa 1890.

African Marigold

Designed by William Morris in 1876.

Wild Tulip

Designed by William Morris in 1884.

Eighteen blocks were used to make up this deceptively simple looking pattern.

Evenlode

Designed by William Morris in 1883.

Morris named many designs after English rivers; the Evenlode is a
tributary of the Thames which has its source in the Cotswolds.

Brother Rabbit

Designed by William Morris in 1883.

Windrush

Designed by William Morris in 1881.

Medway

Designed by William Morris in 1883.

Wey

Designed by William Morris in 1883.

Wey was originally an indigo-discharged printed cotton. Indigo discharge printing is an ancient technique which Morris often used because of the sharpness of line it produced.

'The true happiness taking a interest in details of

secret of
lies in
genuine
all the
daily life.'

Powdered

Designed by William Morris in 1874.

The background of *Powdered* features the Willow motif which Morris uses in several designs.

Peacock and Dragon

Designed by William Morris in 1878.

This design originally had a very large repeat, reaching over a metre tall, and was a fabric intended to be used as a wallcovering.

Wandle

Designed by William Morris in 1884.

This design is named after the river Wandle. William Morris's factory, Merton Abbey Mills, was located on the banks of the river.

Yare

Designed by John Henry Dearle in 1892. This was originally a black-printed cotton.

Strawberry Thief

Designed by William Morris in 1883.

Morris based this design on the thrushes that stole strawberries from his kitchen garden in Kelmscott Manor.

Rose

Designed by William Morris in 1883.

Dove and Rose

Designed by William Morris in 1879.

Corncockle

Designed by William Morris in 1883.

The Corncockle is a British wildflower which, although thought to be extinct, has recently been discovered growing again.

Millefleurs

Designed by John Henry Dearle circa 1912.

This fabric was originally hand-woven on a jacquard loom.

Indian Pink

Designed by John Henry Dearle circa 1918.

Fruit

Designed by William Morris in 1864.

Along with *Daisy* and *Trellis*, *Fruit* formed part of Morris's first ever collection of wallpapers.

Honeysuckle

Designed by May Morris in 1876.

Honeysuckle is one of several wallpapers designed by May, Morris's youngest daughter who ran the embroidery section of The Firm.

Pimpernel

Designed by William Morris in 1876.

This design hung on the wall of Morris's dining room in his London home, Kelmscott House.

Pink and Poppy

Designed by William Morris in 1880.

Seaweed

Designed by John Henry Dearle circa 1890.

Snakeshead

Designed by William Morris in 1876.

Snakeshead, which is named after the meadow flower, shows the influence of Indian textiles on Morris's work. He particularly admired them because they were printed using the natural dyes he so favoured.

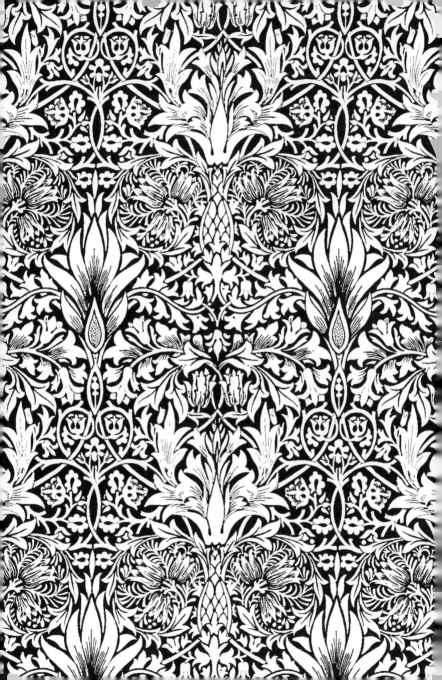

Sunflower

Designed by William Morris in 1879.

Sunflower only contains two colours so was a cheaper paper to produce than many others that Morris & Co. produced.

'History has the kings and because they art has the people, they created.'

remembered
warriors,
destroyed;
remembered
because

5 7 9 10 8 6 4

Hutchinson
20 Vauxhall Bridge Road
London SW1V 2SA

Hutchinson is part of the Penguin Random House
group of companies whose addresses can be found at
global.penguinrandomhouse.com.

Penguin
Random House
UK

First published in the UK by Hutchinson in 2016

www.penguin.co.uk

A CIP catalogue record for this book is available from
the British Library.

ISBN 9781786330437

Printed and bound in Thailand by Sirivatana Interprint

Penguin Random House is committed to a sustainable
future for our business, our readers and our planet.
This book is made from Forest Stewardship Council®
certified paper.

MIX
Paper from
responsible sources
FSC® C018179